Simplified Piano Solo

THE WORLD'S GREAT CLASSICAL MUSIC

MW00561822

Favorite Classical Themes

63 Selections from Symphonies, Ballets, Oratorios & Other Concert Works

Transcribed for Simplified Piano Solo / Lower Intermediate Level

EDITED BY BLAKE NEELY AND RICHARD WALTERS

Cover Painting: DeWhitte, *Interior*, 1668

ISBN 0-634-00212-0

7777 W. BLUEMOUND RD. P.O. BOX 13819 MILWAUKEE, WI 53213

CONTENTS

ABOUT THE COMPOSERS...

TOMASO ALBINONI (1671-1751).

The son of a wealthy paper merchant, Albinoni never needed to look for the sort of court appointments or church positions that sustained his colleagues. Albinoni produced over fifty operas, a number of other stage works, as well as over forty solo cantatas. Bach found some of Albinoni's melodies so compelling that he based several of his keyboard fugues on them. Most of Albinoni's work is similar in sound and texture to that of his contemporary Vivaldi. Yet the "Adagio in G Minor," the piece for which he is most famous, is strikingly unlike his other compositions. Shortly after World War II, Italian musicologist Remo Giazotto discovered a sketchy score of the piece in a Dresden library, including only a bass line and bits of a violin part. Giazatto reconstructed the piece for strings and organ.

JOHANN SEBASTIAN BACH (1685-1750).

Johann Sebastian Bach's incomparable genius for musical form and structure is revered more than 300 years after his birth. Yet the Baroque master and his music were actually forgotten by the general public and musicians alike for many years. Musical fashions were already changing by Bach's later years, and his music was heard less frequently than earlier in his life-time. After his death, which may have been hastened by treatments and surgery for blindness, his music fell out of fashion. His second wife, Anna Magdelena, died in poverty about ten years later. Bach's works span a wide range of genres. He wrote liturgical works, Lutheran masses, church and secular cantatas, chamber music, organ works, orchestral pieces, concer-tos, vocal and choral pieces as well as compositions for clavier. In his day he was widely known as a virtuoso organist. His improvisational skills were legendary. With his contempo-rary George Frideric Handel, whom he never met, he was one of the last great composers of the Baroque era. Some ninety years after Bach's death, his works were once again brought before the public by the composer and conductor Felix Mendelssohn. Mendelssohn became a champion of the works of Bach and other composers who had been pushed aside with the shifting of musical fashions. Bach's music has been a mainstay of the international repertoire ever since.

LUDWIG VAN BEETHOVEN (1770-1827).

It is difficult to know how much of our perception of Beethoven is myth and how much is fact. He was the greatest composer of his era, certainly. Beethoven began his musical studies with his father, a Bonn court musician. He was appointed as deputy court organist in Bonn when he was eleven years old. He later continued his studies with Haydn, until differences between the two ended their relationship. Beethoven was first known to the public as a bril-liant, flamboyant piano virtuoso, but there was a much darker aspect to his life. He was dev-astated when, in his late teens, he was summoned home from Vienna to keep vigil at his mother's deathbed. The second great tragedy of his life began when he was quite young, as a slight hearing impairment. In 1802, when the composer was 32, he was informed by doctors that he would eventually lose his hearing altogether. Beethoven sank into a deep despair, during which he wrote a will of sorts to his brothers. Whether or not he was considering sui-cide is a subject of some speculation. Whatever the case, the "Heiligenstadt Testament," as the will is known, states that he believed he would soon be dead. He eventually came to terms with his deafness and went on to write some of his most powerful pieces. His last six symphonies were written in the following years. In addition to his nine symphonies, Beethoven wrote pieces in nearly every imaginable genre. His works include an oratorio, two ballets, an opera, incidental music for various theatrical productions, military music, cantatas, a wealth of chamber music, 32 piano sonatas, various piano pieces, some 85 songs and 170 folk-song arrangements. At Beethoven's funeral, on March 29, 1827, some 10,000 people joined in his funeral procession. One of the torch-bearers was composer Franz Schubert, who had idolized Beethoven. Some 45 years after his funeral, Beethoven's body was moved to the Vienna's Central Cemetery, where he lies near the grave of Schubert.

JOHANNES BRAHMS (1833-1897).

Johannes Brahms was a man of strong opinions. He disapproved of the "New German School" of composers, namely Liszt and Wagner. He avoided what he believed to be the excesses of the tone poem, relying instead on traditional symphonic forms. After his Symphony No. 1 was premiered, he was hailed as "Beethoven's true heir." The symphony, written when Brahms was forty-three years old, is so clearly linked to the symphonies of Beethoven that it has jokingly been called "Beethoven's Tenth." Brahms began his musical studies as a youngster, gaining experience in composition and working as an arranger for his father's light orchestra. He revered composer Robert Schumann. On the advice of Franz Liszt he met Schumann, with whom he developed a close friendship. He also developed a deep love for Schumann's wife Clara Wieck Schumann. From the time of Schumann's mental breakdown until his death in 1856, Brahms and Clara tended to the ailing composer. The truth of the relationship between Brahms and Clara Schumann remains something of a mystery. Brahms never married. Clara Schumann never re-married following Robert's death. When Clara Schumann died in May of 1896, Brahms did not get to the funeral due to a missed train connection. He died the following April. Throughout his life, Brahms would sign letters "Frei aber froh" (Free but happy), until his last years when he signed "Frei aber einsam," (Free but lonely). One of the pall-bearers at Brahms' funeral was the composer Antonín Dvořák.

CLAUDE DEBUSSY (1862-1918).

Claude Debussy saw rules as things to be tested. He repeatedly failed harmony exams during his student years, because of his refusal to accept that the rules were correct. Like many before him he took several tries to win the Prix de Rome. Debussy's musical language was affected by the music of Wagner, which he heard first-hand at the Bayreuth Festival, and Russian music. Another important event was exposure to the hazy harmonies of Javanese music. Yet the voice that he found was completely French. His music was as much a part of the Impressionist school of thought as the work of any painter. The composer also found his voice in periodic writings as a music critic. By breaking rules and composing in a style uniquely his own, Debussy led the way for a generation of French composers. With his "Prelude to the Afternoon of a Faun" Debussy challenged listeners to discern subtle colors of sound and gently shifting harmonies. When Debussy died, after a long and painful battle with cancer, it seemed as though no one noticed. In fact, France was too consumed with war in 1918 to pause for the death of a composer, even the most important composer in the country.

ANTONÍN DVORÁK (1841-1904).

Antonín Dvorák's parents were firm believers that a child must learn to play an instrument and sing. Dvorák's father, an innkeeper by trade, was an avid amateur musician who played in the town band in Bohemia. But a career in music was unthinkable. The young Dvorák was expected to follow in his father's trade. After many battles the young musician was finally allowed to enter music school. After finishing his studies he took a job in an opera orchestra, taking on private students as well. By his mid-thirties he was supporting himself in great part with his compositions. Brahms, who later became his friend, helped him find a publisher for his work. His fame gradually spread throughout Europe and from there to the U.S. In 1885 Dvorák was invited to become director of the National Conservatory of Music in New York City. In his homeland, Dvorák had been both a fan and a student of folk music. In America he delightedly found a new style of folk music to study. He was particularly taken with the African-American spiritual. Yet he was homesick while in New York. Eventually he found a small Bohemian settlement in Spillville, Iowa, where he could spend his summers speaking his native tongue and generally relaxing in familiar cultural surroundings. In Spillville he worked on his Symphony No. 9, "From the New World." It was premiered in New York in 1893 and was a huge success. In 1895 homesickness took Dvorák back to Prague, where he became director of the Prague Conservatory. He continued to compose, but the disatrous premiere of his opera *Armida* in March of 1904 hurt him deeply. Two months later he died suddenly while eating dinner.

GABRIEL FAURÉ (1845-1924).

Like Beethoven, Gabriel Fauré suffered a gradual loss of hearing which he endeavored to keep a secret from both friends and colleagues. While many remained unaware of his deafness until after his death, his closest friends guessed the situation and ignored the composer's increasingly obvious condition. Fauré was widely respected during his lifetime as an organist and teacher. He was the director of the Paris Conservatory for many years, teaching composition to an entire generation of French composers. Among his pupils were Maurice Ravel and Nadia Boulanger, who would become the most influential composition teacher of the twentieth century. As one might suppose, Fauré had little time left over to devote to his compositional endeavors once his teaching and performing obligations were fulfilled. Summer holidays were his most productive times. He also had little time for romance, entering a marriage of convenience in his early forties. Fauré sought a distinctive voice in his compositions. Although he eventually found a delicate, restrained and understated style, it was slow to be appreciated by the public. He is now regarded as the greatest composer of French song. "Après un rêve" is part of a set of three songs that was written in about 1865. Dedicated to one Mme. Marguerite Baugnies, it is a setting of a text by Romain Bussine.

CÉSAR FRANCK (1822-1890).

Belgian-born César Franck was largely overlooked during his lifetime, at least as a composer. After receiving his education in France, and spending his career there as well, he was awarded the ribbon of the Chevalier of the Legion of Honor from the French government for his work as a professor of organ. There was no mention of his compositions. Franck's father was a banker who, unlike the fathers of most aspiring musicians, actually wanted a career in music for his son. He was delighted when, at age eleven, his son began touring as a virtuoso pianist. He was far less delighted when it became apparent that his son was bound for obscurity as a church organist and composer. Although he was respected as a performer and teacher throughout his life, he had to wait until he was sixty-eight for his first real success as a composer. It was the premiere of his String Quartet in D Major that brought him this public acclaim. In 1879 he was publicly snubbed when only two of the guests he invited to hear the premiere of his oratorio actually attended. Franck was deeply religious and took great pleasure in his service to the church as an organist. The premiere of his Symphony in D Minor, one of his enduring works, was a failure. The orchestra objected to his including the English horn in a symphony and looked disdainfully on a piece by an organ professor. Franck sought to write Romantic music within a Classical framework. He loved to juxtapose diverse sounding instruments. "Panis angelicus," a sacred piece, was composed in the early eighteen-seventies for tenor, organ, harp, cello and double bass.

FRANÇOIS-JOSEPH GOSSEC (1734-1829).

It is a testament to the fickle nature of history that François Gossec is remembered for little other than his "Gavotte." The little piece, charming as it is, is hardly a fair representation of a composer who wrote some 50 symphonies and 20 stage works, founded several prominent performing ensembles and was highly regarded a teacher. Born to a South Netherlands farmer, Gossec displayed his musical talents as a youngster. The story has been told that when the composer was herding cows as a child, he made a violin out of a wooden shoe, using horsehair for strings. In fact, Gossec's symphonies were extremely significant in the development of French symphonic style, and his ballets and comic operas were highly successful. His serious operas, however, were decided failures. During the French Revolution he conducted the Garde Nationale band and wrote a great number of Revolutionary pieces. He was one of the first French composers to use the clarinet in the orchestra and successfully experimented with the effect of hidden antiphonal choirs of singers or instrumentalists.

CHARLES GOUNOD (1818-1893).

While French composer Charles Gounod was in Rome competing for the Prix de Rome, which he won on his third try in 1839, he discovered sixteenth-century polyphonic music wafting about the Sistine Chapel. He was so moved by this music, and likely by the setting as well, that he considered becoming a priest. Instead, he began composing masses and worked as a church organist in Paris. When he began writing operas, he leaned heavily on the examples of Gluck and Meyerbeer. Although these first operas were failures, he soon found his own voice, creating the likes of *Roméo et Juliette* and *Faust*. With *Faust* he struck a blow for French composers. *Faust*, although not a resounding success at the outset, was a powerful opera that came from the pen of a Frenchman. The opera put a dent in the domination of foreign operas in Paris and opened doors for other aspiring French composers. In the fifty years that followed, *Faust* was performed some two thousand times in Paris alone. It was the opera that opened the new Metropolitan Opera Company in New York in 1883. Gounod weathered the Franco-Prussian war living in England, becoming the first conductor of the Royal Albert Hall Choral Society. He returned to Paris in 1875, where he continued to work on operas. From 1881 to the end of his life he wrote almost exclusively church music. Like Mozart, he began a requiem that would prove to be his own. He was sitting at the piano, working on the Requiem, when he slumped onto the keyboard. He died three days later. Gounod's "Funeral March of a Marionette," written in 1873, is best known to television audiences as the Alfred Hitchcock theme.

EDVARD GRIEG (1843-1907).

Edvard Grieg holds a unique position in music history as not just the most famous of Norwegian composers, but as one of the only Norwegian composers to have achieved an international reputation. Grieg drew upon traditional Norwegian folk songs for the inspiration and basis for many of his pieces. His incorporation of national folk music into classical forms inspired musicians throughout Europe to do the same with the traditional music of their own countries. Although Grieg's Piano Concerto in A Minor is his best known work, it is not typical of style. Most of his pieces are small in scale, giving him a reputation as a miniaturist. Grieg's first music lessons came from his mother. When Norwegian violinist Ole Bull heard the teen-aged Grieg play the piano, he arranged for him to enter the Leipzig Conservatory in Germany. Although the young musician was terribly homesick, living so far from home, he enjoyed the opportunity to hear performances by such luminaries as Clara Schumann and Richard Wagner. After his studies in Germany, and later in Denmark, Grieg returned to Norway. Finding himself in demand throughout Europe, Grieg spent much of his career traveling. The recipient of honorary degrees from Cambridge and Oxford, Grieg was also honored as one of his country's foremost composers.

GEORGE FRIDERIC HANDEL (1685-1759).

George Frideric Handel had the good sense to find a receptive audience for his music. Born Georg Händel, in Halle, Germany, the composer defied his father's wishes that he pursue law. He became known as a skilled keyboard player and respectable composer, and became a friend of the composer Georg Philipp Telemann. When his operas were not particularly well received in Hamburg, Händel moved on to Italy. In 1711 he moved on once again, this time to England. Two weeks after his arrival, the spectacle of his opera *Rinaldo* made him a famous man. The composer became a British citizen, changing the spelling of his name to suit his new nationality. The move to Britain proved fruitful, but life was not without its hardships. In 1715 he plunged from the height of success and popularity to absolute ruin. He not only survived, but rebuilt his reputation and once again achieved success. When it became apparent that he was played out as a composer of operas, he turned his attention to the oratorio, finding even greater success there than he had with his operas. He eventually lost his eyesight, which meant the end of his career as a composer. By then, his name firmly established, he turned his attention to conducting and performing as an organist. *Messiah*, certainly Handel's most famous work, composed in 1742, was both the last piece of music he would conduct and the last he would hear. He collapsed shortly after conducting a Good Friday performance of the seventeen-year-old oratorio. He died the following morning. According to his wishes, he was buried in Westminister Abbey. A statue at his grave depicts him in front of his desk, with a quill pen in front of him. Lying on the desk is a score of *Messiah*, open to the soprano aria, "I Know That My Redeemer Liveth."

FRANZ JOSEPH HAYDN (1732-1809).

Born into the Baroque era, Franz Joseph Haydn came of age in the Classical era. He functioned as a trailblazer, making the way for the likes of Beethoven, who was his student. He is remembered as the "father" of the modern symphony and the string quartet for his hand in establishing the forms of both. He was born to poor circumstances, yet his family saw his obvious talent and sent him to a nearby town to live in the home of a music teacher. Although life in his teacher's home was harsh, Haydn was well taught. He went on to sing in the boy choir of St. Stephan's, where he remained until his voice broke at age seventeen. Once on his own, the young musician took a garret apartment and began working as a freelance musician, playing the violin and keyboard instruments and composing. He was eventually offered a court position, which he kept for a short time. When the Esterházy family, one of the most prominent Hungarian families, offered him a job as Vice-Kapellmeister, he immediately accepted. He remained in the employ of the Esterházy family for three decades, becoming full Kapellmeister in 1766. After the death of Nikolaus Esterházy, Haydn was granted a great deal of freedom to travel and to compose for persons other than the Esterházy family. Haydn wrote an astounding amount of music. He penned operas, chamber works, sacred music, over one hundred symphonies, as well as oratorios and even puppet operas. He was so prolific that even though his music is still frequently performed and his name is a household word in the world of classical music, the majority of his work remains unpublished and unknown.

GUSTAV MAHLER (1860-1911).

Gustav Mahler was not exactly a musician's musician. His perfectionism caused him to alienate many of the musicians with whom he worked. When he became music director of the Vienna Royal Opera he cleaned house, replacing orchestral singers and orchestral musicians. He restaged existing productions, seeing to every detail of the productions himself. The musicians considered him heavy-handed, while the opera's management felt he was spending money wildly. Mahler was a workaholic. He devoted his summers to composition since his conducting schedule during the concert season was non-stop. As a composer he devoted his energy entirely to songs, song cycles and symphonies. The symphonies are enormous, involved, Romantic works. They were brutally treated by the critics of his day. His symphonies did not find receptive audiences until after World War II, when they found unprecedented success. Mahler left the Vienna Royal Opera, sailing for New York to conduct at the Metropolitan Opera. While in New York he became instrumental in the revitalization of the New York Philharmonic. But his inability to slow down was taking its toll. Mahler had been warned that his heart was weak and was told to cut back on his working hours. Cutting back was impossible. He worked at his usual feverish pace until he collapsed in New York on February 21, 1911. Unable to return to work, he was moved to Paris for treatments. When it became apparent that he would not recover, he asked to be moved to Vienna where he died on May 18, 1911. The story has been told that in his last hours he conducted an imaginary orchestra with a single finger. It has also been said that his last word was "Mozart."

FELIX MENDELSSOHN (1809-1847).

While most of Mendelssohn's colleagues could tell stories of their battles with family over choice of career and even more tales of their financial struggles as musicians, Felix Mendelssohn could only listen. He was born into a wealthy family that supported his goals in music from the very first. Even in their conversion from Judaism to Christianity, which the family had long considered, they were spurred to action by thoughts of their son's future. It was at the time of their conversion that they changed the family surname to Mendelssohn-Bartholdy. Mendelssohn set out on his musical career with two clear goals. He wanted to re-introduce the largely forgotten music of old masters such as Bach to the public, and he dreamed of opening a first-rate conservatory. At the age of twenty he conducted a pioneering performance of Bach's *St. Matthew Passion*, the first of many such concerts he would lead. A few years later he founded and directed the Leipzig Conservatory. As a composer, Mendelssohn combined the expressive ideals of the Romantics with the traditional forms of the Classical era. He is remembered both as one of the great Romantic composers and one of the last of classicists. In his career Mendelssohn found success at an early age, and remained highly successful until his death. His sister Fanny, to whom he was exceptionally close, died suddenly on May 14, 1847. Shortly after he got the news of his sister's death, Mendelssohn fell unconscious, having burst a blood vessel in his head. Although he recovered from this incident, he was terribly diminished by the illness. His health and mental state deteriorated until his death on November 4 that same year. Memorial services for the great conductor/composer were held in most German cities, as well as in various cities in Great Britain, where he had become quite a celebrity.

JEAN-JOSEPH MOURET (1682-1738).

An accomplished singer and a composer of both vocal and instrumental music, Jean-Joseph was tremendously popular in his day. The son of a silk merchant, who was also known as an amateur violinist, Mouret wrote nine operas and ballets and over 400 divertissements for plays. His controversial opera-ballet *Les fêtes ou Le triomphe de Thalie* (1714) was among the first French operas to employ comedy. In addition to music for the theater, he also wrote motets, cantatas, cantatilles, airs and instrumental works. Among the many positions he held during his musical career, he directed the orchestra of the Paris Opera from 1714-1718. In 1717 he began to work as composer-director with the New Italian Opera in Paris, a position in which he would hold for twenty years. He continued singing, securing an appointment as a singer of the king's chamber in 1720. He functioned as the artistic director of the Concert Spirituel from 1728-1734, for which he composed many of his motets, cantatas and can-tatielles. For many years Mouret enjoyed tremendous popularity and professional accolades. His success faded, however. In the course of just a few years he lost all of his professional positions as well his financial security. By 1737 he was destitute, relying on the charity of friends. That same year his mental health began to fail. In April of 1738 he was sent to an asylum, where he died the following December.

WOLFGANG AMADEUS MOZART (1756-1791).

It is exceptional for nature to produce such a prodigy as Mozart. Playing capably at age three, composing at five and concertizing throughout Europe at age six, Mozart was clearly remarkable, even for a prodigy. But for nature to have placed two prodigies in one household is beyond belief. Mozart's sister Marianne (Nannerl), a few years older than Mozart, was also a prodigy and was also featured on these concert tours. The young musician's parents moved heaven and earth to further offer Mozart every opportunity to perform and study abroad. They traveled Europe incessantly. As an adult, Mozart had difficulties in his relationships with his employers, and with colleagues. Pop culture has presented us with a caricature image of the composer, thanks in great part to the film *Amadeus*, in which he is painted as a freakish, spoiled child that refused to grow up. He was, in fact, impetuous and, likely as a result of his star status as a child, often difficult to deal with. But there was more depth of personality and musicianship than the film attempted to convey. Mozart was known to complete an entire symphony in a single carriage ride, yet he chafed at accusations that it was not work for him to compose. Another factor in the exaggerated stories of his character was his inability to handle financial matters. Although he was well paid for many of his compositions, he was in constant financial difficulty. He was frequently forced to borrow money from family and friends. Mozart, who more than any other composer represents the Classical era, tried his hand at virtually every musical genre available, and succeeded across the board. In 1791 Mozart received a commission to compose a requiem. According to the terms, the source of the commission was to remain anonymous. The piece proved to be the composer's own requiem, in that he died of a "fever" before it was completed. The circumstance of his death, and the anonymous Requiem commission, gave rise to great speculation at the time, and a film some two centuries later. In the mid-twentieth century, the composer Richard Strauss is said to have laid a hand on a copy of Mozart's Clarinet Quintet and said, " I would give anything to have written this."

JACQUES OFFENBACH (1819-1880).

One of the finest tune-smiths of the nineteenth century, Jacques Offenbach helped define the genre of operetta. The international popularity of his operettas paved the way for the creations of such composers Franz Lehár, Victor Herbert and the team of Gilbert and Sullivan. The operettas of Offenbach and others formed the roots of twentieth-century musical theater. Offenbach was raised in France, although his family was German in origin. Offenbach began his musical life with studies on the violin, switching to cello at a young age. Although his comic operas were a tremendous success both in France and abroad during the 1860s, the French civil war of 1870-71 triggered a change in musical taste. Following the war, Offenbach's operettas were no longer the rage they had once been. In 1876, in an effort to make some much needed money, Offenbach embarked on a tour of the United States. He played some forty concerts in the U.S., writing a book on his impressions of America upon his return to France. At the time of his death, Offenbach had completed 95 operettas and comic operas. He also wrote numerous vocal pieces and works for cello, as well as five ballets, additional dance music, vaudevilles and incidental music. Many of his operettas contain sharply witty lyrics that are punctuated by fairly blatant musical effects. Two of Offenbach's operas were unfinished at the time of his death. *Belle Lurette* was completed by Delibes, while his one serious opera, *Les Contes d'Hoffmann* (The Tales of Hoffmann), was completed by Guiraud. *Les Contes d'Hoffmann* is considered his masterpiece, still popular with opera companies throughout the world today.

JOHANN PACHELBEL (1653-1706).

Johann Pachelbel was a renowned organist, composer and teacher. Although his studies and early career took him to various locales, he eventually returned to Nuremberg, the city of his birth, where he served as the organist of St. Sebaldus Church. Among his pupils was one Johann Christoph Bach, the older brother of Johann Sebastian Bach. Pachelbel's other relationship to Bach was a similar interest in experimenting with elaborate variations on the chorale fugue. Pachelbel composed some seventy chorales and ninety fugues over the course of his career. Although the "Canon in D" is by far his most famous work, he wrote very little chamber music of this type.

HUBERT PARRY (1848-1918).

To look at Hubert Parry's academic records from Oxford, one would hardly expect that the young man would come to be known and respected as a composer and music teacher. In his Oxford days he was far more interested in studies and sports than in anything musical. The musician was the son of an arts patron, who had made a name for himself as an avid amateur painter. Parry is said to have begun composing chants and hymns at the age of eight. He was publishing church music, piano pieces and songs as early as the 1860s. Many of his early compositions were destroyed, some say intentionally. He eventually taught at the Royal Conservatory of Music and became the institution's director in 1894. In 1900 Parry began teaching at Oxford. He was a highly respected, intelligent man who used his social standing to invigorate English musical life. Parry wrote a great number of unison songs over the course of his career, one of which is the now famous, "Jerusalem," set to a poem of William Blake.

NIKOLAY RIMSKY-KORSAKOV (1844-1908).

Trained as an officer in the Russian Navy, composer Rimsky-Korsakov had a great interest in music but little training beyond piano lessons. Although he displayed prodigious talents as a child, his aristocratic standing meant that a career in music was out of the question. Yet, after teaching himself counterpoint and harmony, and establishing himself as a composer, he became a professor at the St. Petersburg Conservatory. He was removed from that position when he publicly condemned the police control over the school and its students. Among his students were Alexander Glazunov and Igor Stravinsky. He is remembered as the central figure of "The Russian Five" (or "The Mighty Five"), a group of composers that included Modest Mussorgsky, Alexander Borodin, César Cui and Mily Balakirev. The group favored a dynamic national style in distinct contrast to the elegant sounds of Tchaikovsky. Rimsky-Korsakov composed more than fifteen operas, numerous choral works and orchestral pieces, a great quantity of vocal music, as well as chamber works and piano pieces. Of this great quantity of music only three orchestral pieces have remained in the classical repertoire: the symphonic suite *Sheherazade* for which he is best remembered, his *Spanish Capriccio* and his *Russian Easter Festival*. Written in 1888, *Sheherazade* is based on vignettes from "Tales of the Arabian Nights."

CAMILLE SAINT-SAËNS (1835-1921).

Like Mozart, Camille Saint-Saëns was the sort of child prodigy that defies logical explanation. Able to read and write at age two, the young Saint-Saëns was composing as a three-year-old and performing recitals by age five. He made his formal debut at age ten, offering to play any of the thirty-two Beethoven piano sonatas from memory as an encore. Throughout his life, Saint-Saëns studied a wide variety of subjects. He was a respected writer in the fields of music, history and science. He was a virtuoso pianist, who played the organ with equal proficiency. Franz Liszt praised him as the world's greatest organist. Saint-Saëns was a prolific composer, writing operas, orchestral pieces, sacred and secular choral music, songs, chamber music and even a couple of pieces for band. In his younger years, the composer was an outspoken proponent of contemporary French compositions. He used his popularity and social standing to advance the careers of other composers, not his own. Yet in his middle and later years he not only ceased to support modern French composers, but became an outspoken opponent of the music of Debussy and later of Stravinsky. Along with Mendelssohn, he is credited with reviving neglected music of the past, bringing the likes of Bach, Handel, Gluck and Mozart before the public. Entitled "a grand zoological fantasy," *Carnival of the Animals* was neither published nor performed during Saint-Saëns' lifetime. This was by his own edict. In addition to characterizations of animals, he includes many musical quotations.

FRANZ SCHUBERT (1797-1828).

The story of Schubert's life reads like a heartbreaking novel. Now hailed as one of the great Romantic composers, not one of Schubert's symphonies was performed during his lifetime. It was five decades after his death before any of them were published. Schubert, the son of a school headmaster, was not a virtuoso musician. Although his musical abilities were readily apparent to his teachers, his inability to perform left him with little means to support himself. He taught in his father's school for a time, but was miserable in that job. Schubert studied with Salieri, who was astounded by the young composer's abilities. After writing his first symphony at age fifteen, Schubert presented Salieri with a completed, fully orchestrated opera two years later. Schubert lived less than thirty-two years, yet he composed a phenomenal amount of music, including some six hundred songs. One hundred and forty-four of those songs date from the year 1815, a year in which he was teaching at his father's school. After Schubert left his father's school, he had the good fortune to collect a small group of devoted friends and supporters. The friends would periodically organize evenings of the composer's music, which came to be known as "Schubertiades." Schubert's health began to fail as early as 1822. When he died at age thirty-one, he was viewed as a composer of songs. It was not the enormous number of songs that earned him this mistaken designation so much as the fact that almost none of his other music had been performed during his lifetime. In addition to the songs, Schubert completed seven symphonies, and left one unfinished. He wrote a number of operas, although these are far from his best works. He also wrote choral works, chamber music and piano pieces. In accordance with his dying wish, he was buried beside Beethoven, whom he had idolized and at whose funeral he served as a torch-bearer.

ROBERT SCHUMANN (1810-1856).

Robert Schumann's dream was to become a pianist. As the son of a German bookseller and writer, he grew up surrounded by literature and instilled with a love of music. His world crumbled however, when he was just sixteen, with the death of his father and the subsequent suicide of his sister. Schumann entered law school, but spent most of his time studying music. In 1830 he moved into the household of his piano teacher, Friedrich Wieck. Soon afterwards, his left hand began to trouble him. His career dreams were shattered when his left hand became permanently crippled. He turned his energies to composition, making a name as a music critic as well. An inspired critic, he founded the music journal Neue Zeitschrift für Musik, in 1834. He often wrote under the pseudonyms "Florestan" and "Eusebius," Schumann fell in love with his teacher's daughter, Clara Wieck, a highly acclaimed concert pianist. Clara's father fought vigorously against the romance. Schumann married Clara in 1840, but only after he had taken his case to the courts. In the year he was married, the composer wrote some 150 songs, turning to orchestral music the following year. Schumann suffered from bouts of terrible depression, which became progressively worse with time. In 1854 he attempted suicide. Unable to function any longer, he was then placed in an asylum, where he spent the last two years of his life. His wife and his friend, the young composer Johannes Brahms, looked after him in those final years.

BEDRICH SMETANA (1824-1884).

Like Beethoven, Smetana did not allow his loss of hearing to stop him from composing, and managed to compose one of his greatest works after his hearing was gone. Smetana's hearing loss, however, was connected to larger health problems that at first affected his memory and speech and in the end robbed him of his sanity. In 1884 he was persuaded to enter an asylum, where he died later that year. He was buried with full Czech honors. Smetana was a child prodigy. After receiving his first music lessons from his father, he began playing in a string quartet at age five and composing by age eight. But, as the son of a brewer, whose fortunes suffered a serious reversal when the composer was a young man, there was little financial support for his musical endeavors. Smetana found himself teaching to support himself, maintaining contacts with such touring musical stars as Franz Liszt and Clara Schumann. The composer's financial instability paled in comparison to his suffering over the loss of three of his four daughters between the years 1854 and 1856. Persuaded by Liszt, the young composer moved to Sweden to try his luck in a new country. From 1856 to 1861, Smetana found himself in demand in Sweden as a composer, pianist and conductor. He eventually returned to Czechoslovakia (then Bohemia) where he began to incorporate traditional folk melodies into his classical compositions. He is remembered as the first great Czech nationalist composer.

JOHANN STRAUSS, JR. (1825-1899).

Just as John Philip Sousa was America's March King, Johann Strauss, Jr. was Austria's Waltz King. The Strauss family is synonymous with the waltz. Johann, Sr. was a violinist, conductor and composer, who was widely popular throughout Europe. He conducted in a flamboyant style, with violin in hand. He popularized the open-air concert and programmed many of his numerous works. His son Josef was also a conductor, working with the family orchestra and composing a number of pieces as well. Eduard, a younger son, became Vienna's imperial-royal music director from 1872-1901. He was the most respected conductor of the Strauss clan, and was in great demand throughout Europe. But it was Johann, Jr. who won the hearts of the Austrian people. His talent was recognized early and his first composition was published when he was only six years old. As an adult, he formed a rival orchestra to his father's and began to tour with his own music. Eventually the two groups were merged into a single family orchestra. While the public loved Johann, Jr., the world of classical music saw him as lacking substance. For all the criticism he received during his lifetime, his music is familiar to classical audiences a century after his death. During Johann, Jr.'s last days, the city of Vienna waited anxiously for hopeful news of his health. On June 3, 1899, a large crowd gathered for an outdoor concert. In mid performance, a messenger bolted onto the stage and whispered something into the conductor's ear. The conductor abruptly stopped the orchestra. After a few moments they began playing the opening notes of "By the Beautiful Blue Danube," Strauss' beloved waltz. The audience knew in an instant what it meant. Their Strauss had died. Rising to their feet, the men removed their hats and bowed their heads while women cried. A few days later, Johann Strauss, Jr.'s obituary referred to him as "the last symbol of cheerful, pleasant times."

PYOTR IL'IICH TCHAIKOVSKY (1840-1893).

It is a curious twist of fate that the composer of so bombastic a work as the *1812 Overture* should have been an extremely fragile individual. Exceptionally sensitive from childhood, Tchaikovsky eventually deteriorated into a precarious emotional state. Tchaikovsky's musical abilities were already quite evident by age five, as was his hypersensitivity. His mother died when he was fourteen, a painful event that some say prompted him to compose. Over the years he was plagued by sexual scandals and episodes we might call "nervous breakdowns" today. Historians have uncovered evidence that his death, which was officially listed as having been caused by cholera, was actually a suicide. Many believe that the composer knowingly drank water tainted with cholera. Tchaikovsky's work stands as some of the most essentially Russian music in the classical repertoire, yet he was not a part of the Russian nationalistic school. In fact, he was treated quite cruelly by critics of his day. "Tchaikovsky's Piano Concerto No. 1, like the first pancake, is a flop," wrote a St. Petersburg critic in 1875. A Boston critic claimed that his Symphony No. 6 ("Pathétique") "...threads all the foul ditches and sewers of human despair; it is as unclean as music can well be." For all the vehement criticism the composer received during his lifetime, his works are now among the best loved of the classical repertoire. His ballet *The Nutcracker* is an international holiday classic, while *Swan Lake* is staple in the repertoire of ballet companies throughout the world. His *1812 Overture* is among the most recognizable of all classical pieces. In 1893 the composer completed work on his Symphony No. 6. The first movement dealt with themes of passion, the second with romance, the third with disillusionment and the finale with death. The piece was premiered on October 28. Nine days later the composer was dead.

GIUSEPPE VERDI (1813-1901).

The son of an innkeeper, Verdi was playing the organ in a local church by the age of seven. His parents were hard-working Italian peasants who bought the young boy a spinet when they realized his musical inclinations. At sixteen he became assistant to the organist of the largest church in the town of Busseto. In 1832, after publishing a few of his songs, he moved to Milan. There he was denied admission to the conservatory because he was found to be "lacking in musical talent." His reception at the conservatory not withstanding, Verdi's opera *Oberto* was performed at La Scala in 1839. The opera's limited success brought him a commission for three more operas at La Scala. After the death of his young wife and the failure of his first comic opera, *Un giorno di regno*, Verdi nearly quit composing in despair. It was the prospect of his opera *Nabucco* that kept him going. In 1842 *Nabucco* became an enormous success, eventually earning Verdi an international reputation. He became wildly popular. Everything from food to toys bore his name. Although the political aspects of some of Verdi's operas are often over-emphasized, he was indeed a political figure. He was eventually elected to the national parliament and later to the senate. With time and many successful operas came great wealth. Verdi had often said that had he not been a composer he would have been a farmer. During his years in elected office, he also tried his hand at farming. For some fifteen years he produced no new operas, but did compose the Requiem. His composition continued into his old age, with his operas *Otello* (1887) and *Falstaff* (1893).

ANTONIO VIVALDI (1678-1741).

Antonio Vivaldi was very nearly forgotten by concert-going audiences until the early part of the twentieth century. It was violin virtuoso Fritz Kreisler who reminded the music world of Vivaldi's music by turning some of his themes into salon pieces. By the end of the twentieth century even those having little knowledge of classical music must have heard Vivaldi's "The Four Seasons" in the context of a motion picture soundtrack or a diamond commercial. Ordained as a priest in 1703, Vivaldi taught at a girls' school in Venice, writing for the orchestra and chorus of the school. He was known as the "red priest" owing to his vivid red hair. Vivaldi exerted a tremendous influence over German musicians, many of whom imitated his style. His creative concerto writing, complete with energetic repeated rhythmic patterns and unusual combinations of solo instruments, was one of his most important contributions. Yet history treated his remarkable output rather roughly. Russian composer Igor Stravinsky once noted that Vivaldi had written "one concerto four hundred times." Considered the "father" of the modern concerto, Vivaldi's plan of three concerto movements (fast-slow-fast) set the standard for generations of composers to come. Vivaldi also wrote a great deal of vocal music, including more than forty operas. By the time of his death, his music had largely fallen out of fashion. He died a pauper, buried outside the Vienna city walls. One of a handful of singers at his funeral was the young Joseph Haydn.

Adagio in G Minor

Tomaso Albinoni
1671-1751
originally for organ and strings

Bist du bei mir
(You are with me)

Johann Sebastian Bach
1685-1750
BWV 508
originally for voice and figured bass

Brandenburg Concerto No. 2 in F Major

First Movement Excerpt

Johann Sebastian Bach
1685-1750
BWV 1047
originally for orchestra

Allegro

Brandenburg Concerto No. 5

First Movement Excerpt

Johann Sebastian Bach
1685-1750
BWV 1050
originally for orchestra

original key: D Major

Jesu, Joy of Man's Desiring

Jesus bleibet meine Freude
from Cantata No. 147, HERZ UND MUND UND TAT UND LEBEN

Johann Sebastian Bach
1685-1750
BWV 147
originally for choir and orchestra

36

Turkish March
from THE RUINS OF ATHENS

Ludwig van Beethoven
1770-1827
Op. 113
originally for orchestra

Piano Concerto No. 5

"Emperor"
First Movement Excerpt

Ludwig van Beethoven
1770-1827
Op. 73
originally for piano and orchestra

original key: E-flat Major

Symphony No. 5 in C Minor
First Movement Excerpt

Ludwig van Beethoven
1770-1827
Op. 67
originally for orchestra

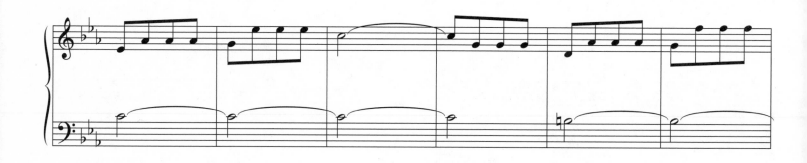

Symphony No. 7 in A Major
Second Movement Excerpt

Ludwig van Beethoven
1770-1827
Op. 92
originally for orchestra

Allegretto

Lullaby
(Wiegenlied)

Johannes Brahms
1830-1897
Op. 49, No. 4
originally for voice and piano

Symphony No. 1 in C Minor
Fourth Movement Excerpt

Johannes Brahms
1830-1897
Op. 68
originally for orchestra

Allegro non troppo ma con brio

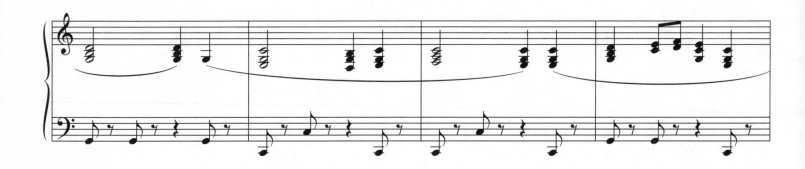

Symphony No. 4 in E Minor
First Movement Excerpt

Johannes Brahms
1830-1897
Op. 98
originally for orchestra

Prelude to the Afternoon of a Faun
(Prélude à l'après-midi d'un faune)
Opening Excerpt

Claude Debussy
1862-1918
originally for orchestra

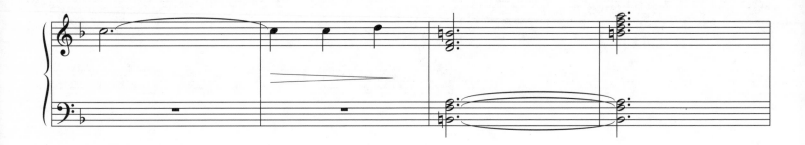

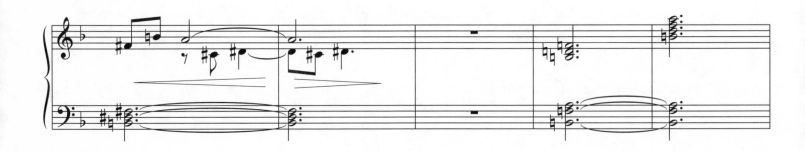

Symphony No. 9 in E Minor

"From the New World"
Second Movement Excerpt ("Largo")

Antonín Dvořák
1841-1904
Op. 95
originally for orchestra

Après un rêve
(After a dream)

Gabriel Fauré
1845-1924
Op. 7, No. 1
originally for voice and piano

Panis angelicus

César Franck
1822-1890
originally for tenor and
instrumental ensemble

Gavotte

François-Joseph Gossec
1734-1829
originally for flute and string quartet

Funeral March of a Marionette
Themes

Charles Gounod
1818-1893
originally for orchestra

In the Hall of the Mountain King

from PEER GYNT

Edvard Grieg
1843-1907
Op. 23, No. 7
originally for orchestra

76

Allegro
from WATER MUSIC

George Frideric Handel
1685-1759
originally for orchestra

Air
from WATER MUSIC

George Frideric Handel
1685-1759
originally for orchestra

Andante con moto

Hallelujah

from the oratorio MESSIAH
Excerpt

George Frideric Handel
1685-1759
originally for chorus and orchestra

Pastoral Symphony
from the oratorio MESSIAH

George Frideric Handel
1685-1759
originally for orchestra

I Know That My Redeemer Liveth

from the oratorio MESSIAH
Excerpt

George Frideric Handel
1685-1759
originally for orchestra

Gypsy Rondo
Keyboard Trio No. 23 in G Major
Third Movement

Franz Joseph Haydn
1732-1809
originally for violin, violoncello, keyboard

Symphony No. 104

"London"
First Movement Excerpt

Franz Joseph Haydn
1732-1809
originally for orchestra

Allegro

original key: D Major

The Heavens Are Telling
from the oratorio THE CREATION

Franz Joseph Haydn
1732-1809
originally for chorus and orchestra

Allegro (♩ = 116)

Trumpet Concerto in E-flat Major
First Movement Excerpt

Franz Joseph Haydn
1732-1809
originally for trumpet and orchestra

Symphony No. 2 in C Minor
"Resurrection"
Fifth Movement Choral Theme

Gustav Mahler
1860-1911
originally for soloists,
chorus and orchestra

Symphony No. 5 in C-sharp Minor
Fourth Movement Excerpt ("Adagietto")

Gustav Mahler
1860-1911
this movement originally
for strings and harp

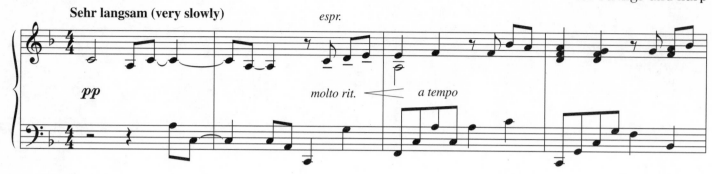

"Fingal's Cave" Overture

or "The Hebrides"
Themes

Felix Mendelssohn
1809-1847
Op. 26
originally for orchestra

Violin Concerto in E Minor
First Movement Excerpt

Felix Mendelssohn
1809-1847
Op. 64
originally for violin and orchestra

Allegro molto appassionato

Rondeau
Excerpt

Jean Joseph Mouret
1682-1738
originally for orchestra

Ave verum corpus

Wolfgang Amadeus Mozart
1756-1791
K 618
originally for chorus and orchestra

Piano Concerto No. 21 in C Major

"Elvira Madigan"
Second Movement Excerpt

Wolfgang Amadeus Mozart
1756-1791
K 467
originally for piano and orchestra

Lacrymosa
from REQUIEM

Wolfgang Amadeus Mozart
1756-1791
K 626
originally for chorus and orchestra

Symphony No. 38
"Prague"
First Movement Excerpt

Wolfgang Amadeus Mozart
1756-1791
K 504
originally for orchestra

original key: D Major

Symphony No. 41 in C Major

"Jupiter"
First Movement Excerpt

Wolfgang Amadeus Mozart
1756-1791
K 551
originally for orchestra

Allegro vivace

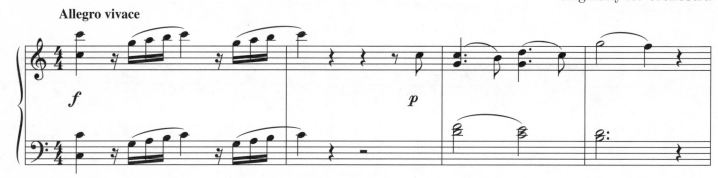

Can Can

from the opera ORPHEUS IN THE UNDERWORLD

Jacques Offenbach
1819-1880
originally for chorus and orchestra

Canon

Excerpt

Johann Pachelbel
1653-1706
originally for 3 violins and continuo

Adagio

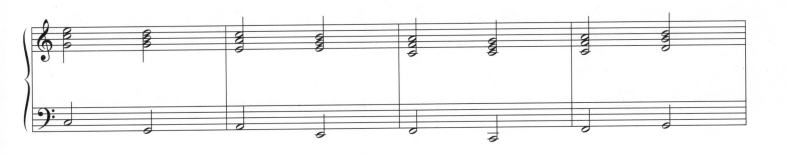

original key: D Major

rit.

Jerusalem

Hubert Parry
1848-1918
originally for chorus and organ

Slow, but with animation

Sheherazade
Themes from Part 1

Nikolay Andreyevich Rimsky-Korsakov
1844-1908
Op. 35
originally for orchestra

The Swan
from the suite THE CARNIVAL OF THE ANIMALS

Camille Saint-Saëns
1835-1921
originally for chamber ensemble

Die Forelle
(The Trout)

Franz Schubert
1797-1828
D 531
originally for voice and piano

Poco moderato

Ave Maria

Franz Schubert
1797-1828
D. 839
originally for voice and piano

Symphony No. 5 in B-flat Major
First Movement Excerpt

Franz Schubert
1797-1828
D 485
originally for orchestra

Ich grolle nicht
(I bear no grudge)

Robert Schumann
1810-1856
Op. 48, No. 7
originally for voice and piano

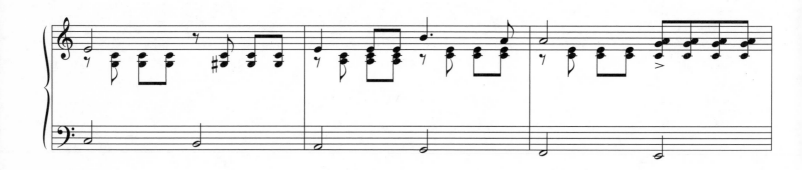

Piano Concerto in A Minor
First Movement Themes

Robert Schumann
1810-1856
Op. 54
originally for piano and orchestra

Allegro affettuoso

168

The Moldau

from the symphonic cycle MÁ VLAST (My Fatherland)
Excerpt

Bedrich Smetana
1824-1884
originally for orchestra

Allegro commodo non agitato

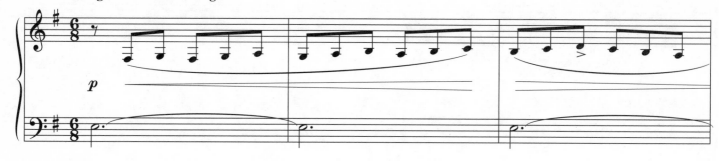

By the Beautiful Blue Danube

Themes

Johann Strauss, Jr.
1825-1899
Op. 317
originally for orchestra

Tempo di Valse

180

Tales from the Vienna Woods
Themes

Johann Strauss, Jr.
1825-1899
Op. 325
originally for orchestra

Copyright © 1999 by HAL LEONARD CORPORATION
International Copyright Secured   All Rights Reserved

1812 Overture

Excerpt

Pyotr Il'yich Tchaikovsky
1840-1893
Op. 49
originally for orchestra

Marche Slav
Themes

Pyotr Il'yich Tchaikovsky
1840-1893
Op. 31
originally for orchestra

Grave quasi marcia funebre

Dance of the Sugar Plum Fairy

from the ballet THE NUTCRACKER

Pyotr Il'yich Tchaikovsky
1840-1893
Op. 71
originally for orchestra

Andante ma non troppo

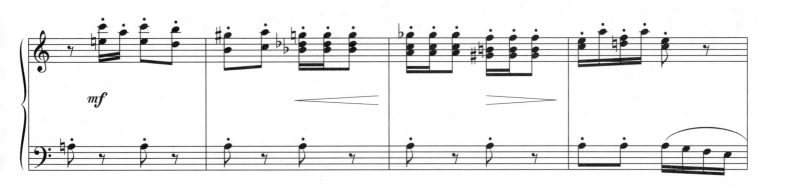

Dance of the Reed-Flutes

from the ballet THE NUTCRACKER

Pyotr Il'yich Tchaikovsky
1840-1893
Op. 71
originally for orchestra

Moderato assai

Dance of the Swans

from the ballet SWAN LAKE

Pyotr Il'yich Tchaikovsky
1840-1893
Op. 20
originally for orchestra

Tempo di Valse

Romeo and Juliet
FANTASY OVERTURE
Excerpt

Pyotr Il'yich Tchaikovsky
1840-1893
originally for orchestra

Symphony No. 6

"Pathétique"
First Movement Excerpt

Pyotr Il'yich Tchaikovsky
1840-1893
Op. 74
originally for orchestra

Andante *veneramente, molto cantabile con espressione*

Moderato assai

original key: B Minor

Violin Concerto
First Movement Excerpt

Pyotr Il'yich Tchaikovsky
1840-1893
Op. 35
originally for violin and orchestra

oiginal key: D Major

Lacrymosa
from REQUIEM

Giuseppe Verdi
1813-1901
originally for soloists, chorus and orchestra

Largo (♩ = 60)

come un lamento

ppp dolciss.

The Four Seasons

"Autumn"
First Movement Excerpt

Antonio Vivaldi
1678-1741
Op. 8, No. 3
originally for violin and orchestra

Gloria in excelsis

from the Mass GLORIA

Antonio Vivaldi
1678-1741
originally for chorus and orchestra

Allegro

220

Mandolin Concerto in C Major
First Movement Excerpt

Antonio Vivaldi
1678-1741
originally for mandolin and orchestra